TUNSIYA / AMRIKIYA

Editors' Selection from the 2017 Frost Place Chapbook Competition

TUNSIYA

AMRIKIYA

poems by

LEILA CHATTI

BULL CITY PRESS

DURHAM, NORTH CAROLINA

TUNSIYA/AMRIKIYA

Published in the United States of America

Library of Congress Cataloging-in-Publication Data

Chatti, Leila
Tunsiya-Amrikiya: poems / by Leila Chatti
p. cm.
ISBN-13: 978-1-4951-7877-1

Book design by Spock and Associates
Cover photos by Leila Chatti

Published by
BULL CITY PRESS
1217 Odyssey Drive
Durham, NC 27713

www.BullCityPress.com

ACKNOWLEDGMENTS

The author would like to thank the editors of the following journals and anthologies, in which these poems first appeared:

Crab Orchard Review: "Cousins"

Ecotone: "Upon Realizing There Are Ghosts in the Water"

Linebreak: "Muslim Christmas"

Narrative Magazine: "Muslim Girlhood," "Fasting in Tunis," "Night Lament in Hergla," "Hometown Nocturne"

Nimrod Journal: "A Religious Education," "Momon Eats an Apple in Summer"

Raleigh Review: "Morning Swim"

Rattle: "My Mother Makes a Religion," "While Reading the News About Orlando, I Hear the Call to Prayer"

The Rumpus: "Motherland"

Virginia Quarterly Review: "When I Tell My Father I Might Begin to Pray Again"

Poems also appeared in the following anthologies: "Spark" in the 2015 *Nazim Hikmet Poetry Competition Anthology,* "What Do Arabs Think of Ghosts?" in *Best New Poets 2015*, "Motherland" in *Best New Poets 2017*, and "While Reading the News About Orlando, I Hear the Call to Prayer" in *Best of the Net 2016* and *Bettering American Poetry 2017*. "Hometown Nocturne" was listed as a special mention in the 2018 Pushcart Prize Anthology.

Deep gratitude to the Creative Writing Program at North Carolina State University, the Munster Literature Centre, the Quest Writer's Conference, Nimrod Conference for Writers and Readers, Dickinson House, the Tin House Writers' Workshop, the Fine Arts Work Center in Provincetown, and the Wisconsin Institute for Creative Writing for their generous funding and support;

Ross White, Noah Stetzer, and the Bull City Press team for everything they've done for me and this work;

Dorianne Laux, Joseph Millar, Mary Szybist, Joy Harjo, Naomi Shihab Nye, Fady Joudah, Anita Skeen, Marianne Forman, and Stephen Esquith for their knowledge, guidance, and boundless encouragement;

Rebecca Bornstein, Carlene Kucharczyk, Tyree Daye, Marty Saunders, Laura Thorp, Dee Lalley, Heather Bowlan, Chelsea Krieg, Elizabeth Purvis, Tayler Heuston, Emily Rose Cole, Emilia Phillips, Matthew Wimberley, Philip Matthews, Zeina Hashem Beck, Kaveh Akbar, Anders Carlson-Wee, and Tiana Clark for friendships that have made me a better writer, thinker, and person;

and Henrik Mader, Bryce Emley, Samuel Piccone, Erin Willie, Lexi Wilson, Elissa Fountain, and Michael Deagler for their particularly steadfast love, patience, and enthusiasm, no matter where we find ourselves in the world. Thank you for believing in me.

3a'ilati, my kin—Rachid, Téfida, Nejib, Danielle, Rached, Cyrine, Myriam, Saloua, Yassine, Riadh, Houda, Sonia, Ferid, Nadia, Mohammed Salah, Inés, Mehdi, Samia, Fakhri, Farah, Lilia, Slim, Hend, Raymond, Eileen, Jeanette, Kathy, Jessica, Lindsey, Paul, Johnny, Patti, Beth, Ken, Dennis, Renée (Rubes), Tom, Kelsey, Haley—and *usrati*, my closest blood—Karim, Pegi, Amina, Rachid, Leith—

this is for you.

CONTENTS

Tunsiya
(Arabic) Tunisian, female.

Amrikiya
(Arabic) American, female.

MUSLIM GIRLHOOD

I never found myself in any pink aisle. There was no box for me
with glossy cellophane like heat and a neat packet of instructions
in six languages. Evenings, I watched TV like a religion
I moderately believed. I watched to see how the others lived, not knowing
I was the Other, no laugh track in my living room, no tidy and punctual
resolution waiting. I took tests in which Jane and William had
so many apples, but never a friend named Khadija. I fasted
through birthday parties and Christmas parties and ate leftover *tajine*
at plastic lunch tables, picked at pepperoni from slices like blemishes
and tried not to complain. I prayed at the wrong times in the wrong
tongue. I hungered for Jell-O and Starbursts and margarine, could read
mono- and diglycerides by five and knew what *gelatin* meant, where it came from.
When I asked for anything good, like Cedar Point or slumber parties,
I offered a quick *inshallah*, as in *Can Jordan sleep over this weekend, inshallah?*,
peeking at my father as if he were a god. Sometimes, I thought
my father was a god, I loved him that much. And the news thought
this was an impossible thing—a Muslim girl who loved her father.
But what did they know of my heart, or my father
who drove fifty miles to buy me a doll like a Barbie
because it looked like me, short brown hair underneath her hijab, unthreatening
breasts and feet flat enough to carry her as far as she wanted
to go? In my games, she traveled and didn't marry, devoured any book
she could curl her small, rigid fingers around. I called her *Amira*
because it was a name like my sister's, though I think her name
was supposed to be *Sara*, that drawled *A* so like *sorry*,
which she never, ever was.

A RELIGIOUS EDUCATION

I learned to be flexible—those positions boys like—
from five daily contortions

into the bathroom sink. I can reach my foot up
and rest it in the basin, can cock my head

to drink from the stream between metal
lip and porcelain bowl.

Watching the men bending
down to pray in their rows, I learned

the intricate curvatures
of the other body: cavern of the throat

calling to God, that O of the mouth.
Each rack of shoulders, each sloped back and mound

of ass, I liked to watch them kneel
and fall forward, kneel and fall forward,

lips hovered just above the rug. There,
I learned my body, too.

Sundays, my hips practiced
their shifting sway, slow

crossing through the men's side to join
my kind. And each year I learned better

to hunger, my stomach a fist, those long days
of fasting, holy month of appetite, ritual of

anticipation. I eyed the men passing,
a starved woman, that ache in me

pulsing, its red mouth hissing *wait, wait, soon.*

FASTING IN TUNIS

Longing, we say, because desire is full
of endless distances.
—ROBERT HASS

My God taught me hunger
is a gift, it sweetens
the meal. All day, I have gone without
because I know at the end I will
eat and be satisfied. In this way,
my desire is bearable.

I endure this day
as I have endured years of days
without the whole of your affection.
Your desire is one capable of rest.
Mine keeps its eyes open, stalks
through heat that quivers,
waits to be fed.

The sun burns a hole through
the sky and I am patient.
The ocean eats and eats
at the sand and still hungers.
I watch its wide blue tongue, knowing
you are on the other side.

What is greater: the distance between
these bodies, or their need?

Noon gapes, a vacant maw—
there is long to go
until the moon is served, white as a plate.
You are far and still sleeping;
the morning has not yet slunk into your bed,
its dreams so vast and solitary.

Once, long ago,
I touched you,
and I will touch you again—
your mouth a song
I remember, your mouth
a sugar I drink.

MY MOTHER MAKES A RELIGION

to replace the old gods. Scripture
gleaned from the backs
of magazines, stars—she follows
horoscopes like commandments,
tells me *Leila, you'll be lucky*
in love this month, but watch out
for the eyes of strangers, whatever that means,
a cigarette waved like a censer
through the air, calligraphy of smoke.
My mother rubs oil for wishes
on her wrists in the dark
aisles of the wiccan shop she loves
so much (*except for the tarot cards and candles*
shaped like dicks, she has limits), and won't pass
any open water without first sinking
in a coin. She insists on fortune
cookies, but only believes
the ones she likes. My mother stays wary
of magic, forbade me late-night
Ouija conversations, but once
paid thirty dollars for a psychic
to summon her sister, then cried.
A child, I heard the trinity wrong—
thought God was a ghost, her faith
a haunting. But now I know God is just
like any man: shifty and often late.
God's like a bad dog that doesn't come
when He's called, and my mother waits
for no one. Summers, her holy
months, she lies by the pool
and anoints her own good self
with her own good sweat. Her wet palms
turn tabloids to birds, the pages ruffled,

as she tilts her face, defiant, toward an empty sky.
In these moments, I'll believe anything
she tells me, still and radiant
as a painting of a saint, halos
in her sunglasses and the future
sleek and spread in her hands—
my mother, Seer of the week ahead,
my mother the miracle that will save herself.

COUSINS

Summers, we became wild,
        scattering

like sand once the moon
        took like a hook

in the sea's dark
        mouth. Our parents swished

smoke on the balcony, doled out
        dinars silver as sardines

and kissed gentle
        warnings past our cheeks.

We entered the streets'
        unspecific dimness, bodies

bumping to be close, arms
        linked and our skin

smelling like jasmine and salt.
        We poured

gossip into the cups of each
        other's ears, sticky breath

in three languages. At the port,
        we wore dappled

light in all colors, lapped palms
        sugared by

cacahuètes and crêpes bought
from carts, dipped

toes in shallows like minnows and sipped
shisha tendrils

and Cokes brown as heaven.
When finally we headed

back home, the stars lit
above us like embers

between the late-night
lips of uncles,

the moon our grandmother,
pale and tucked in.

We sang club hits to each other
like lullabies, whispering

Ces soirées-là! as the bougainvillea
nodded in the breeze, vivid

as dreams, and the strays
slunk from our shadows

and laid down to sleep.

DRIVING TO HERGLA DURING RAMADAN

We hide the water.
Take covert sips and tuck

the bottle between the seats.
Outside, miles

of sand and the air
trembling as if nervous.

I watch the olive trees flicker
by in neat rows, observe

the silent congregation.
Because it is the holiest

month, we pretend
to be pious—listen

to an orchestral CD we find
in the glove box, then

the radio's endless
Qur'anic recitations, nothing else

with words. Near Hergla,
at a tollbooth, a man peddling home-

made bread, round and flat
as a plate. No window

rolls down. Like them,
we drive on, have someplace

to be. In the rearview,
I catch him

sway in the blistering heat.

MOMON EATS AN APPLE IN SUMMER

She keeps each sliver
to herself. Her fingers draw

the blade through the flesh
up to the bed of her thumb

and stop
and there is no blood—she knows

not the day or my name, but this,
how to slice through

safely, understands
still the realm of pain.

Her face, old fruit
left in a bowl

washed with sun.
Her name the echo

of apple—*tafahah*, *Téfida*.
She sings it

like a chant,
calls through each room of the house

Téfida, Téfida, Téfida,
searching for herself.

She pares the fruit
down to its tough spine,

the apple dismantled, the skin
stripped into green half moons

placed in a shallow dish, their bellies
the color of teeth, of bone.

HOMOPHONES

In English, *alter*
and *altar* are so similar
they are easily confused.

Uttered her name to
herself over and over.

My grandmother,
altered, made
an altar.

Adrift through vacant
rooms, wasting.

The Tunisian word
for asleep is *rek'ked*,
which sounds like *wrecked*.

My grandmother swaying
unawake, a boat sinking.

At some point, *morning*
linked inextricably to *mourning*.

Sun bobbing up from horizon, shaking
off night's black water.

As *peace* exists now
as *piece*, partial.

Found erected in a splash
of light the altar: silver
comb, jasmine bunch, pistachio
husks sucked clean.

In Tunisian, *death* is
moot—unsettled, uncertain, no longer
worth the dispute.

At the center, a photograph:
all seven children
lined up, fading.

FARQ

When my grandmother died, I flew an ocean
to grieve her. On the phone with my father, I tried to
puzzle it out—she was dead, but she was dead
in the future, five hours ahead, there was still time
for goodbyes, last kisses and murmurs past cheeks, here
she would still be breathing.
The day I left, magnolias dripped
onto Raleigh's streets as if thawing, and the spring sun shrugged
off winter's grip. Clouds
frothed outside the plane's porthole windows and dawn
spilled toward me, a flush of light.
It was April and everything glowed
pink and alive. But in Tunis, it was as if
I'd alighted, stunned, into another
world where all was dry—dust
on marble and jasmine
desiccated brown on the dashboard
of the rented car, hot as a mouth.
The highway shimmered, coughed up shivery
air like ghosts. We passed
the olive groves, rows of silver-green
leaves and hunched spines, miles of sand
blanched beneath the sky so clear
God could easily look through it
if He wanted. My father, who hadn't prayed
in years, played the Qur'an from a cassette tape
and said nothing. I didn't
know yet the rules of death
in this country—all my life considered it refuge
from my American tragedies, a grief-
less sanctuary. So when we arrived,
my grandmother already tucked in
the arid earth like an unviable seed
three days earlier, I didn't expect the crush

of distant relatives and neighbors I knew vaguely
by face, crowded on the white terrace of her
house smoking cigarettes, wailing or shuffling
with their hands shoved in their pockets
or lifting tiny cups of Turkish coffee to their mouths.
It was Lilia, the youngest of the daughters
now orphaned, still round-faced at fifty
like a child, who pressed her lips to my cheeks
and said *farq*, which I did not understand until her son
illumed—*separation*, ritual
day of acknowledging the death and life
ever after as changed, *different, a division*
between what was and what is, now
that the loved one is gone. And what I felt
then was a flood of something like relief,
to have my grief charted for me—three days
of mourning; on the third day, letting go—
and so I let the ululations of near-
strangers wash over me from hallways, the salon, the grounds
where once she watched her progeny
collect coiled husks of snails
like coins, pluck hibiscus and plant them
behind ears like flamenco dancers, dip
toes into the blue mosaicked pool. I let myself be
carried from room to room with my dozen cousins
as if by a current, said the requisite prayers, said *Inna lillahi*—
etcetera, my tongue stumbling, my still-living heart
welling up like an eye. And when at the end
of the day, the aunts ordered
us into the showers one by one, *to wash off*
the death, we obliged—the emptying
house dewy, filling with steam. All night, a lulling,
ubiquitous hiss.

MORNING SWIM

Because my father asks me to, I rise
in the freshly broken heat. We meet
silently like co-conspirators, a towel slung
across his shoulders like a shawl,
then trek through the unforgiving
sun of this country, one that raised
my father brown and speckled, gave him
his god and tongue. But there is no balm
either can offer, joint failure of language
and prayer—the ones we love sleep across the ocean
and do not miss us. We walk toward it,
swish of sand beneath our *shlakas*, desert
barbs grazing pink our tender ankles
as flies dot the sky like ellipses.
The heat licks us and leaves its animal
scent, salt sheened over every inch.
Cresting a dune, first glimpse of sea, its water
green and neat. We shed our human
burdens on the shore, rubber flip-flops
and towels abandoned in a heap,
then linger in the littoral grit.
Early light shears cleanly through, glints off
shells and shoals of pewter fish. We approach
the blue skin of horizon, surface
smooth as a bed's new sheet, everything still
and untroubled around us, the ocean
parting gently as we enter, then sealing us in.

WHEN I TELL MY FATHER I MIGHT BEGIN TO PRAY AGAIN

He says he's never really stopped
speaking to God. Says it's in his DNA, asking
for things.

Twenty-one years he bowed before the bed, us
children in a row behind him
crushing our foreheads earnestly to the floor.

I can't remember the last time
I clasped my hands above my breast and yearned for
God in that formal way,

but my father possesses an exact date—
Christmas, seven years back, the final *jummah*,
after which he walked out into the blinding

snow. *O ye who believe*! If there exists
in my blood a map, it is one I keep
folded for fear

of where it does not lead. God,
I want so badly
to speak

with you—not for aid or for proof of
my goodness, but to feel
again your presence

in my life, undeniably there
like my father's hand on mine
in this still and inscrutable dark.

NIGHT LAMENT IN HERGLA

This is what the fearful do:
when a burning star torments them, they go to the sea.
—MAHMOUD DARWISH

There is no world in which I am not haunted,
no willing God to relinquish me.
My mother taught me death comes
wailing from the shadows, my father
all ghosts exist in smoke. I search
the sky for light long extinguished,
make wishes on their bright graves.
In the dark I try every language you might
recognize, but nothing calls you back;
the words hang in the air, their own
brief phantoms. The ocean offers
no solace; I stand at its black edge
as it retreats, draws close, backs away again.
Like this, your memory wavers
in the threshold. How many nights
your name appeared on my lips
like an incantation, how many times
you've arrived in a dream pale
as prayer at dawn—your absence
burns its hole through my waking.
I stalk the shores of your sleep,
which allow no entry. The moon
reveals nothing of heaven, a brined window.
You are gone, in this country and all others.

WHAT DO ARABS THINK OF GHOSTS?

I think the woman means Muslims—ghost
of a word mixed up with our bodies, as if they were
the same thing—but either way I have no answer.
I haven't asked around. There is too much
death—it swells our tongues. It chokes.
The soul is a bird flying; it doesn't rest long
and its language is different. There are three
nightjars preening under the evening's cloak,
by which I mean three souls. Are souls clean?
Are ghosts? If every sad death made
a phantom, my country would be thick with them,
we would breathe them like air, they would keep us living.
What do ghosts think of Arabs, I want to know—
our fires blooming like invasive blossoms, bombs
planted like bulbs awaiting the spring?
Death grows here. There are more every day.
Before she died, my grandmother could
only say her name. I don't know the names
of the dead accumulating like snowflakes, so many
the news talks about them as if they are one thing,
a mound of indistinguishable parts. Who
calls for them, who houses them in their mouths?
In skies blue as a door, the metal ghosts soar:
they have wings but are no bird, have no soul.
We know this better than anyone.

UPON REALIZING THERE ARE GHOSTS IN THE WATER

—in memory of the refugees drowned crossing the Mediterranean Sea

I should have known but the water
never told me. It sealed its blue lips
after swallowing you, it licked my ankles
like a dog. I won't lie
and say the ocean begged for forgiveness;
it gleams unchanged in the sun.
Some things are so big they take and take
and remain exactly the same size.
Darkness is like this; grief too. I cry
and the ocean slips from me—all along
a little sea roiling inside with its own
sad phantoms. For a summer I soaked in
its green warmth, wore its salt like gemstones.
Now the heavy shame: how I waded in
to your grave as if trying it on,
how, when the waves came,
they gave me back.

WHILE READING THE NEWS ABOUT ORLANDO, I HEAR THE CALL TO PRAYER

Not metaphor, but outside
the window, the muezzin
calling from town, his voice faint
as a phantom arrived in the room.
How many times have I felt
shame at those words—*Allahu*
akbar—felt it twist
like a knife inside me?
Once, lonely, I listened
for hours to recordings
of the *adhan* through
Macbook speakers,
wept and knew myself
in the presence of God.
My God, during this all holy
month, when I am so far
everything back home
seems like a dream, its violence
only a wakeable sleep—
where are you to refuse those
who call out to you, who undo
what you've made in your name?
I am not asleep and they are
not waking. Again there is blood
on the floor in your name
and there is no god
but you, so answer.

SPARK

—for Mohamed Bouazizi

As a child, they made us fear
cigarette butts and firecrackers

which, when dropped, would catch
everything ablaze. We watched

the flames swallow Californian forests whole,
eying with suspicion the flickering

birthday candle, the onyx cord,
the candent bulb of the lamp.

When you ignited, they gave you
two minutes' mention on American news

before switching to holiday sales, those red suits
and snowflakes falling like ash.

A December so still I swear I could hear the snap—
match against stone, hiss of life—

and everywhere I looked, fleeting
pinpricks of light, solitary embers burning,

air choked already with smoke.

KHOUYA

(Tunisian Arabic) *my brother*

On the train to Berkeley, a boy
with lashes so thick I felt an ache
for my brother. And he could have been
my blood, his brows knit together
over an iPhone bold as my own
proud sprouts, our skin twin
olive shades. I try to explain this
to my boyfriend after, lounging in bed,
his pale limbs intertwined
with mine—how I search every face
for the familiar, wish simultaneously
to watch over and be watched,
to feel in this country protected by some
semblance of kin. So it breaks
my heart when, later
that day, I read another story
of another man who could have been
my blood, killed, his blood
spilled while his family watched,
the mouth behind the gun
saying *dirty*, meaning someone
like me, or my brother.
And I think of how, at the masjid,
we call everyone *brother* because it is possible
to love a stranger that much.
I just don't see it, how anyone could
look through hate like a scope at boys
so like my brother—somewhere
unknown to me, likely watched
by another as he hunches over
a glowing screen, the pitch-
dark of his eyes and his lashes
so thick, each time he blinks
they fan against his cheeks like wings.

MOTHERLAND

What kind of world will we leave
                    for our mothers? My mother

calls me, weeping. I am
                    far and the country she gave

me could kill me. Or
                    that's what she's saying, her voice

clumsy with tears—my mother
                    who never cries, and so

for this, too, apologizes. Sometimes, more
                    often, I want to mother

my mother. I've begun to
                    wonder what it is like for her

to have four hearts
                    outside her body, buried

in brown and fragile skin. *I never wanted this*
                    for my children, my mother sobs

from a Michigan town
                    where once men crowded in white

cloaks, their sons still
                    there lingering at drug stores and gas pumps

with steely guns and colder eyes.
                    What do you tell a mother

you love too much
                    to lie to? My mother

named me Leila because it was a song
                    white men played on air guitars, which meant,

she'd hoped, they couldn't hate me. *I'm so scared now*
for Rachid, even with his blonde hair—

My mother thought her blood
might protect us in this country

from this country, her fair genes and cast-
aside Catholic god. Thinks now

she failed us as children because she only ever told us
stories of monsters

we wouldn't recognize. Mother,
I know these men

could be your brothers
and do not blame you. She weeps.

I am far and the country
monstrous. What kind of world

do we mother, knowing
what it is, what it's capable of?

The long night stretches
between her window and mine.

As if comforting a child, I say the word
kind—as in, *the world is still*

kinder than we think. I think
I believe it. *Mom* I say

stop crying—no one's leaving this world
to anyone yet.

OKAY WHEN ARE WE GOING

They're not coming to this country if I'm president. And if Obama has brought some to this country they are leaving, they're going, they're gone.

—PRESIDENTIAL CANDIDATE DONALD TRUMP
ON MUSLIMS ENTERING THE UNITED STATES

My mother says to us, over pasta, *Okay, when are we going*
to talk about the elephant in the room? We're at a restaurant,
me and my sister and our Arab father wedged between our white
boyfriends and, at the far end, our brothers who've darkened
like berries with time. At first we don't know
what she means, butter knife gripped in her fist like a spear,
but then she spits it out, voice lowered, as if it's obscene—
Trump—and all of us swallow, even if our mouths are empty.
What I knew, before, of the word was little—something
to do with wielding a winning hand in a game
I was unprepared to play. And I suppose I've always felt
that way: placed just outside a circle I was desperate
and hoping to join. My father, when he came to this country,
carried with him his passport, his god, and a handful
of words like coins. My mother taught him her tongue, which I understood
as love. And understood, too, when, that summer after the towers sank
like a heart, she pinned the tiny striated flag to my breast
before my flight back *there*, the other land, as though it might protect me
from this one. My mother, looking the same
as she does now, white-lipped and terrified, in a Midwestern restaurant
ten days 'til Christmas, snow fluttering past the window
like flakes of ash. That summer, back where she could not reach us,
they lined us up like stars—splayed us with toes and fingers touching,
my brothers six and five. I was a child. I cried. The flag shuddered on my chest.

MUSLIM CHRISTMAS

It sat downstairs on the air hockey table,
its shedding needled branches, its copper wire arms.
With care, our mother draped its false twigs in silver
garlands, two for a dollar on the clearance rack,
and the ornaments—her mother's, long dead—
we cradled in our palms like baby Jesus might have
been held, our non-savior swathed in hay in the barn-crib, safe
and human. Before the two-foot tree,
we made our own, traced our hands on green construction paper,
cut out five-fingered fronds and taped them to the wall.
Our mother wept at its absurdity. But each December
he came for us, there were glittering gifts beneath
whatever false icon we had constructed, and I marveled at how
merciful this man-God could be, Santa Christ, Saint Jesus,
who had found our home and come before the altar
of the unbelieving, stood there in its wavering light,
and left for us chocolate, snow boots, everything we liked.

HOMETOWN NOCTURNE

When I can't sleep, I remember it: blue fields
of night I'd slip into, my borrowed coat
and secondhand boots trailing frayed laces
through curbside sleet and neighbors' lawns,
the poplars lanky and indifferent as teenagers,
the moon a spitball on the back of heaven's
dark shirt. Some nights a boy would wait
in a car humming down the street, thumbs
drumming the wheel and the tailpipe panting.
But more often the ones I liked didn't drive, got all As
and ran cross-country, had parents that kept them
from me, tongued my name like a secret
sweet. A good Muslim girl, I kissed mostly
above the belt, prayed when I had to, and when I slid
lipstick into my sleeve at the drugstore I felt bad about it,
I was very good at feeling bad. The sky fell regularly
in little white stars that caught in my hair. The air
singed my lungs, exhaled as tinsel. I shadowed
streets heading nowhere, asphalt erased
beneath a fresh sheet, season of rimed windows
and bated breath by the radio. In every living room,
some kind of nocturnal glow—plastic menorahs'
tongues of flame, cheap bulbs burning in fir branches,
a nightlight shaped like a man of snow or God.
And in darker rooms our parents fell asleep
on their backs watching reruns, our brothers
clicked on videos of squirming blondes in the trembling
glare of computer screens, while somewhere else,
in a bar or basement, prized Midwestern jewels gleamed
in the bellies of college girls, Burnett's
swirling in a cup and the tiny planets
of ping-pong balls circling Solo rims.
Like this, I orbited the town of my origin,

slogged familiar paths of salt-marbled sidewalks,
ringed cul-de-sacs and parking lots and potholes'
gritty ice rinks. The hooded eyes of houses
looked on and past me. The huddled trees
whispered, brandished pompoms just for show.
I carved carefully my name in frost.
Scuffed my feet the whole way home.

NOTES

In "Muslim Girlhood," mono- and digylcerides and gelatin are mentioned because they are sometimes sourced from pork, and are thus considered forbidden in Islam.

The epigraph for "Fasting in Tunis" comes from the Robert Hass poem "Meditation at Lagunitas."

"Cousins" borrows a line from the song of the same name by the French singer Yannick.

"Momon," in "Momon Eats an Apple in Summer," is a family nickname derived from the French grand-maman (grandmother). The poem is in memory of my grandmother, Téfida Hafsia.

"Farq" describes a Tunisian funerary tradition. Named for the Arabic word meaning "separation," the ritual takes place on the third day following a death. Separate from the burial and viewing of the body, which happens during the first two days, Farq instead marks the acceptance of the deceased's departure from this world and the beginning of a gradual return to daily life. Visitors are received until evening without invitation, at which point the family privately shares a meal.

In "When I Tell My Father I Might Begin to Pray Again," the line "O ye who believe!" comes from the Qur'anic verse (62:9) referencing the *jummah* (Friday prayer).

The epigraph for "Night Lament in Hergla" comes from Mahmoud Darwish's poem "The Strangers' Picnic," translated by Munir Akash, Carolyn Forché, Sinan Antoon, and Amira El-Zein.

The line "skies blue as a door" in "What Do Arabs Think of Ghosts?" refers to traditional Tunisian architecture, which commonly features large, ornate blue doors.

In 2016, over 5,000 refugees and migrants died crossing the Mediterranean Sea. Between Libya and Italy, the likelihood of dying was one death for every 47 arrivals. The poem "Upon Realizing There Are Ghosts in the Water" is in memory of these lives, and the lives lost before and since, in what is an ongoing tragedy.

"While Reading the News About Orlando, I Hear the Call to Prayer" is written in response to the Pulse nightclub shooting on June 12th, 2016. The attack, committed by a Muslim assailant, occurred during the holy month of Ramadan. The poem contains references to the *adhan*, the Muslim call to prayer: the opening ("Allahu Akbar") and the closing ("There is no god but God.").

"Spark" is in memory of Mohamed Bouazizi, a Tunisian street vendor whose self-immolation in December of 2010 sparked the Tunisian Revolution, and thus the entire Arab Spring.

"Khouya" responds to the 2016 murder of Khalid Jabara in Tulsa, Oklahoma, by his neighbor, who referred to Jabara's family as "dirty Arabs."

"Motherland" was written in response and resistance to the 2016 presidential election of Donald Trump.

The epigraph for "Okay When Are We Going" is a quote from Donald Trump made during the Republican presidential debate on December 15th, 2016.

"Hometown Nocturne" pays homage to my hometown—East Lansing, Michigan.

GLOSSARY OF TERMS

Adhan: the Muslim call to prayer.

Allahu akbar: (Arabic) God is the greatest.

Cacahuètes: (French) peanuts. As street food, typically roasted in sugar.

Dinar: the currency of Tunisia.

Farq: (Arabic) separation. A Tunisian funerary tradition occuring on the third day following a death.

Hergla: a small town in northeastern Tunisia, off the Gulf of Hammamet.

Hijab: a head-covering worn in public by some Muslim women.

Inna lillahi wa inna ilayhi raji'un: (Arabic) "Surely we belong to God and to Him we shall return." A verse from the Qur'an recited by Muslims during hardship or tragedy, especially in response to a death.

Inshallah: (Arabic) God willing.

Jummah: also known as Friday prayer, a congregational prayer held every Friday at noon.

Khouya: (Tunisian Arabic) my brother. Used colloquially for friends or kind strangers.

Masjid: (Arabic) mosque.

Muezzin: the man appointed at a mosque to recite the call to prayer.

Shisha: hookah.

Shlakas: (Tunisian Arabic) flip-flops.

Tafahah: (Arabic) apple.

Tajine: a baked Tunisian egg dish similar to a frittata.

Tunis: the capital of Tunisia.